SPIRITUAL DILEMMAS

Deeper Reflections

120 Would-You-Rather Prompts for Intuition, Healing & Psychic Awakening

Lewis Mabee

Spiritual Dilemmas: Deeper Reflections

Paperback Edition

Copyright © 2025 Lewis Mabee

All rights reserved. No part of this publication may be reproduced, stored in a retrieval system, or transmitted in any form or by any means—electronic, mechanical, photocopying, recording, or otherwise—without prior written permission of the author, except for brief quotations used in reviews or scholarly works.

ISBN: 978-1-0696649-2-1 (paperback)

This book is offered for inspiration and entertainment. It is not intended as a substitute for professional medical, psychological, legal, or financial advice. The author makes no guarantees regarding outcomes from practices or reflections contained herein. Always seek the advice of qualified professionals where appropriate.

First Edition

Table of Contents

Introduction 4
Chapter 1: Past Lives & Future Insight 9
Chapter 2: Energy Awareness & Perception 23
Chapter 3: Spiritual Practices & Tools 37
Chapter 4: Healing & Empathy 51
Chapter 5: Guidance & Intuition 65
Chapter 6: Elemental & Earth Wisdom 79
Chapter 7: Cosmic Connection & Universal Wisdom 93
Chapter 8: Self-Discovery & Conscious Creation 107
Chapter 9: Time, Legacy & Identity 121
Chapter 10: Spiritual Service & Mission 135
A Thank You from Lewis 148
About the Author 148
Resources & Next Steps 149
One Small Favor that Helps Immensely 149

Introduction

Spiritual Dilemmas: Deeper Reflections

Welcome, curious soul.

If the first book invited you to tiptoe into wonder, this one asks you to step all the way in—to stretch your thinking, soften your edges, and listen for the wisdom that hums beneath everyday life. Spiritual Dilemmas: Deeper Reflections is a playful doorway into serious growth: a book of "Would-You-Rather" prompts designed to spark laughter and brave inner work, to widen perception and ground you in practical insight.

Think of each dilemma as a tiny ceremony. Two choices. One you. And between them—a field of awareness where intuition, compassion, and courage can meet.

What this book will do for you

Deepen your intuition. By imagining yourself inside each scenario, you rehearse subtle sensing: clairsentience, clairvoyance, inner knowing. Over time, your "gut" becomes a trustworthy instrument.

Expand perception. These questions gently challenge assumptions about energy, time, and connection—stretching the boundaries of what you've believed possible.

Strengthen emotional and spiritual resilience. The reflections help you learn from your own answers, not mine. You'll see where you default to fear, where you lead with love, and where you're ready to evolve.

Create meaningful connections. Used with friends, clients, or circles, the prompts ignite conversations that move beyond small talk—without losing warmth or humor.

Support soulful journalling. The built-in reflections are crafted to pull deeper threads, so your journal becomes a mirror, a map, and a safe place to practice being more you.

Why "Would You Rather" works (spiritually and scientifically)

Our brains love choices. Present the mind with two vivid options and it lights up: values, memories, and instincts all jostle forward. Add the lens of spirituality—energy, symbol, archetype—and those choices become oracles. Your answer is rarely about which option is "right." It's about what your choice reveals: your priorities, permissions, longing, and limits. That insight is gold.

And yes, humor helps. Laughter softens the ego's grip and opens a wider window for guidance to slip through. This is deep work in playful clothing.

What to expect as you read

A clear rhythm: each prompt offers two paths; each reflection invites you to slow down and notice why you chose what you chose.

Varied terrain: intuition, mediumship, healing, elemental wisdom, cosmic connection, service, legacy—this book roams widely (on purpose). Life is not one note.

Gentle edge-walking: some questions will feel deliciously easy; others may feel prickly. That prickle is a growth signal—breathe, stay kind, keep going.

Glimmers of humor: because Light speaks fluent laughter. Expect the occasional wink from the Universe.

How to use this book (solo practice)

- ✽ Arrive. One long breath. Shoulders down. Hand on heart or belly.
- ✽ Choose a prompt. Open at random or follow the chapter path.
- ✽ Feel before you think. Notice your body's instant "this one." That sensation is data.
- ✽ Journal the reflection. Answer the follow-up questions on paper. Write past the obvious. If you surprise yourself, you're doing it right.
- ✽ Integrate. End with one line: "Because of this insight, I will…" (make a call, set a boundary, rest, forgive, explore, celebrate).

With a friend or circle

- ✸ Create a container. One candle. Phones away. A shared intention to explore with kindness and curiosity.

- ✸ Take turns. One person reads a dilemma; everyone chooses silently, then shares their "why."

- ✸ Listen to learn, not to fix. No debate club. Curiosity questions only: "What did that choice represent for you?"

- ✸ Close with gratitude. Name one insight you're taking with you.

A few friendly principles

- ✸ Your truth, your timing. There are no correct answers here. If a question feels too spicy today, skip it and come back later.

- ✸ Ethics matter. Power without compassion is noise. If a prompt raises questions about consent, boundaries, or the right use of ability, good. Explore them. This is how we grow safe, skillful practitioners and communities.

- ✸ Bodies first. If a scenario stirs big feelings, pause to regulate: breathe, sip water, step outside. Spiritual work honors the nervous system.

- ✸ Play is sacred. Joy is not a detour; it's a path. Let yourself giggle, groan, roll your eyes, and be delightfully human.

If you're brand-new (and if you're seasoned)

- ✸ New to the path? Start with the chapters that feel inviting. Use the reflections to practice noticing sensation, symbol, and story. Your only job is to notice without judgment.

- ✸ Experienced practitioner? Treat the dilemmas as calibration tools. Where do you still outsource authority? What edges are ready for refinement? Which gifts want more room?

A short invocation before you begin

May these pages be a playground for wonder and a sanctuary for truth.

May your curiosity be brave, your discernment kind, and your laughter loud enough to loosen what is heavy.

May every choice reveal more of who you really are—

and may that knowing ripple out as healing, peace, and joyful service.

Turn the page. Choose a path. Then another. Let the questions do their quiet work. The Universe is already leaning in, smiling.

Chapter 1:

Past Lives & Future Insight

Would you rather...

Sit down with your inner elder for five candid minutes,

OR

shadow your inner beginner for a full day without interfering?

∽ Reflection ∾

Which relationship—wise advisor or curious apprentice—would most shift your choices now?

Would you rather...

Borrow unshakable patience from your inner elder,

fearless momentum from your inner pioneer?

 Reflection

Which quality would actually move you today?

Would you rather...

Remember the exact promise you made before incarnating,

OR

forget the promise and feel unshakable trust in life anyway?

୨୦ Reflection ୧୧

Is clarity or surrender the kinder compass for you today?

Would you rather...

Watch the blooper reel of your karmic lessons,

OR

see the director's cut where you nailed them on the first take?

∽ Reflection ∾

How does humor help you integrate what you'd rather hide?

Would you rather...

Meet the first soul you'll mentor next lifetime,

OR

reconnect with the last guide who mentored you in the previous one?

⸎ Reflection ⸎

Does gratitude expand you more facing forward or looking back?

Would you rather...

Carry a calendar that highlights "destiny days,"

wear shoes that only walk you toward aligned choices?

℘ Reflection ℘

Do you rely more on planning or embodiment to stay on purpose?

Would you rather...

Download a perfectly linear life-purpose map,

OR

wander a spiral path guaranteed to deliver meaningful synchronicities?

৵ Reflection ৻

Do straight lines or spirals feel more trustworthy to your soul?

Would you rather...

Retire one unhelpful life story you keep repeating,

 OR

double your rest and let your nervous system write a kinder one?

 Reflection

Which path feels safer and more sustainable—mental edit or embodied reset?

Would you rather...

Merge with a future version of you who has forgiven everything,

embrace a past version who still needs your compassion?

 Reflection

Which reunion heals the present you more completely?

Would you rather...

Stand at the threshold of your next breakthrough,

OR

linger at the doorway of a lesson you've finally outgrown?

℘ Reflection ℘

Which threshold gives you the clearest instructions for now?

Would you rather...

Be assigned a cosmic proofreader who edits your thoughts before you speak,

OR

be accompanied by a cosmic comedian who lightens every serious conversation?

⚘ Reflection ⚘

Where do you most need grace right now—precision or levity?

Would you rather...

Glimpse the moment humanity chooses love en masse,

OR

notice the quiet instant you choose love instead of being right?

❧ Reflection ☙

Which scale of miracle are you truly willing to practice?

Chapter 2:
Energy Awareness & Perception

Would you rather...

Host a seance with great-grandparents you never met,

OR

meet the great-great-grandchild you'll never hold?

ꙮ Reflection ꙮ

Past roots and future branches both shape identity—where does your curiosity flow first?

Would you rather...

Cleanse your energy field with a roaring bonfire on a starry beach,

OR

with a silent walk through an old-growth forest after rain?

～ Reflection ～

Fire and water, sound and hush—what elements restore you most effectively?

Would you rather...

Give up all divination tools except a single deck of oracle cards,

OR

abandon cards entirely and rely solely on deep inner seeing?

✥ Reflection ✥

Tools and intuition dance together—how much scaffolding do you truly need?

Would you rather...

Witness one reality-bending sign in broad daylight,

OR

track a trail of small, precise synchronicities all month?

⸙ Reflection ⸘

Which kind of proof helps you trust more consistently?

Would you rather...

Send healing light into the collective grief of humanity,

OR

concentrate it on one specific person who mirrors your younger self?

ꕤ Reflection ꕥ

Macro and micro healing both ripple outward—where does your compassion feel most potent today?

Would you rather...

Perceive the story beneath someone's words with crisp clarity,

OR

sense the need beneath their actions with tender accuracy?

✎ Reflection ✎

Which lens would you steward more ethically?

Would you rather...

Spend a night in a haunted Victorian manor to document spirit activity,

⟡R

camp beneath meteor showers to commune with star beings?

∽ Reflection ∾

Earthbound souls and cosmic kin each widen perspective—whose company thrills (or chills) you more?

Would you rather...

Heal by singing an otherworldly chant,

OR

by weaving silent mudras in the air?

ঌ Reflection এ

Sound and gesture channel frequencies differently—what channel feels most natural in your body?

Would you rather...

Possess perfect recall of every past-life lesson,

OR

forget them all but keep the earned wisdom embodied?

ᛞ Reflection ᛞ

Memory can instruct, yet embodied knowing may suffice—how much narrative do you need?

Would you rather...

Mentor one prodigy who exceeds your abilities,

# OR

empower thousands who reach competence?

 Reflection

Depth versus breadth—what legacy resonates with your soul's blueprint?

Would you rather...

Merge with the consciousness of the Moon during eclipses,

OR

with the Sun during solstices?

✎ Reflection ✎

Shadow integration and illumination both serve wholeness—which dance calls this year?

Would you rather...

Heal through laughter yoga that spontaneously channels,

OR

through stillness that radiates silent grace?

Reflection

Motion and quiet seed harmony—where do you access the deepest flow?

Chapter 3:
Spiritual Practices & Tools

Would you rather...

Glimpse the exact moment your life purpose is fulfilled,

OR

live without ever seeing that timestamp?

ಈ Reflection ಲ

Knowing the ending can anchor focus, or steal spontaneity—which risk feels lighter?

Would you rather...

Carry a pocket stone that absorbs negativity but needs monthly burial,

OR

wear a pendant that amplifies love yet makes you weep when others suffer?

∽ Reflection ∾

Every gift bears a cost—what trade-off aligns with your capacity?

Would you rather...

Align your circadian rhythm to lunar phases,

OR

to planetary hours?

ৎ Reflection ൞

Cycles within cycles—which cosmic clock would most harmonize your lifestyle?

Would you rather...

Learn every herbal remedy known to ancient healers,

OR

decode the vibrational medicine of modern sound therapy?

⁕ Reflection ⁕

Past wisdom and future tech both heal—where does your curiosity sprout?

Would you rather...

Experience clairalience so keen you smell every emotion,

OR

clairsentience so deep you feel every tingle of spirit touch?

✧ Reflection ✧

Sensory expansion can delight or overload—how would you manage the influx?

Would you rather...

Time-travel for thirty minutes to witness Atlantis at its peak,

OR

Lemuria in its final sunrise?

⸙ Reflection ⸙

Lost civilizations carry echoes of collective memory—what message might you bring back?

Would you rather...

Hold a real-time dialogue with pollinators in a garden,

OR

sit in slow conversation with an ancient grove?

❧ Reflection ☙

Fast messages or deep messages—which serves you now?

Would you rather...

See the energetic cord between all the people you love,

OR

the karmic knot that challenges you most?

✾ Reflection ✾

Connection and lesson coexist—which sight would transform you today?

Would you rather...

Have dreams that predict world events with 70% accuracy,

OR

dreams that reveal your personal path with 90% clarity?

∽ Reflection ⁓

Collective foresight and personal guidance both carry responsibility—which weight feels right?

Would you rather...

Receive spontaneous Reiki each time you hear laughter,

OR

each time you hear rainfall?

～ Reflection ～

Joy and cleansing both spark renewal—which trigger suits your environment?

Would you rather...

Open a portal to meet your star family for five minutes,

OR

to meet your Earth soul tribe for five hours?

❦ Reflection ❧

Cosmic origin and earthly kin both ground identity—whose hug do you crave?

Would you rather...

Manifest success via perfectly timed synchronicities,

OR

via steady incremental alignment you can track?

∽ Reflection ∾

Quantum leaps and stepwise climbs both reach summits—what pace honors your nervous system?

Chapter 4:
Healing & Empathy

Would you rather...

Offer silence that lets someone find their own answer,

OR

offer words that name what they can't say?

◈ Reflection ◈

Which gift empowers them more without taking their power?

Would you rather...

Briefly feel another's pain in your body to locate it,

OR

keep your field clear but see a precise map of where it lives?

❦ Reflection ❦

Empathy and discernment protect healing differently—where do you draw the line?

Would you rather...

Receive every apology you were owed,

OR

offer every apology you still owe?

❦ Reflection ❧

Which direction of repair would actually free your heart today?

Would you rather...

Be the person people call at 3 a.m.,

OR

become the teacher who makes those calls unnecessary?

✼ Reflection ✼

Support and skill-building serve love—which role sustains you?

Would you rather...

Cook a simple meal that steadies someone's nervous system,

OR

hold a quiet vigil that steadies their spirit?

⚡ Reflection ⚡

Body and soul co-regulate—where is your medicine strongest?

Would you rather...

Carry boundaries that others instantly recognize,

OR

radiate compassion that softens defenses on contact?

℘ Reflection ℘

Protection and openness are both medicine—what balance keeps you honest?

Would you rather...

Unravel a generational pattern in your family line,

OR

dissolve the same pattern in your wider community?

⟨⟩ Reflection ⟨⟩

Personal and collective healing interweave—where does your effort ripple widest?

Would you rather...

Know exactly what your body needs to heal each morning,

OR

know exactly what to offer the next person you meet?

❥ Reflection ❦

Self-tending and service are twins—who needs your precision first?

Would you rather...

Mirror someone's emotion perfectly until they feel seen,

OR

anchor steady neutrality until they feel safe?

℘ Reflection ℘

Co-regulation has many tones—what does this moment ask of you?

Would you rather...

Remember the first moment a wound took root with tenderness,

OR

imagine the last moment it still mattered and let it go?

❧ Reflection ☙

Origin and closure both liberate—where is your doorway?

Would you rather...

Forgive someone who will never understand the harm,

OR

request a repair conversation that might be messy?

✺ Reflection ✺

Inner release and outer accountability serve different truths—which aligns with your integrity now?

Would you rather...

Sit beside a stranger in visible pain for an hour,

OR

spend that hour calling a relative you find difficult?

❧ Reflection ❧

Comforting the unknown and repairing the familiar both stretch the heart—where is your brave edge?

Chapter 5:
Guidance & Intuition

Would you rather...

Act on a quiet nudge that arrives mid-conversation,

OR

wait for confirmation after you're alone?

❦ Reflection ❦

Do you trust yourself under social pressure, or only in solitude—what does that reveal about sovereignty?

Would you rather...

Let guidance speak through temperature shifts (warm/cool),

OR

through color flashes behind closed eyes?

ঔ Reflection ঔ

Somatic and visual channels teach differently—which sense is easiest for you to honor consistently?

Would you rather...

Keep a daily "three signs I ignored" log,

OR

a "one tiny nudge I honored" log?

❦ Reflection ❦

Does growth come faster by studying misses or by reinforcing wins—where does your brain learn best?

Would you rather...

Receive a single clear sentence each morning,

 R

a wordless knowing that arrives at random times?

 Reflection

Language can soothe doubt; felt sense can bypass it—what form builds real trust for you?

Would you rather...

Establish a personal yes-symbol that appears within 24 hours,

OR

a body signal that fires instantly?

❧ Reflection ☙

External confirmation and internal calibration both guide—where do you want the authority to live?

Would you rather...

Be advised by an inner council of archetypes,

OR

by one steady inner mentor?

❦ Reflection ❦

Many voices bring nuance; one voice brings focus—what governance style fits your psyche now?

Would you rather...

Spot "fear dressed as intuition" every time,

 R

never need to know why your guidance is right?

Reflection

Transparency grows discernment; surrender grows faith—what would mature you more today?

Would you rather...

Get timing as an exact minute ("act at 3:17 pm"),

OR

as a clear window ("before the weekend")?

❦ Reflection ❧

Precision can create pressure; flexibility can invite drift—what tempo keeps you aligned?

Would you rather...

Follow guidance that benefits you but confuses others,

OR

guidance that's explainable but asks for more patience?

❧ Reflection ☙

Acceptance from others and patience from self are both prices—what currency can you afford?

Would you rather...

Heed a nudge that contradicts your plan but aligns with your values,

OR

one that confirms your plan but stretches your comfort zone?

❦ Reflection ❧

Values and growth both demand courage—what kind do you have in stock today?

Would you rather...

Share your guidance openly and risk eye-rolls,

OR

keep it private and let results speak?

✤ Reflection ✤

Visibility tests courage; privacy tests trust—where is your edge?

Would you rather...

Trade some accuracy for limitless compassion,

OR

keep high accuracy with ordinary bedside manner?

❧ Reflection ☙

Skill without heart can wound; heart without skill can mislead—what balance best serves the work?

Chapter 6:
Elemental & Earth Wisdom

Would you rather...

Learn weather-whispering to invite gentle, healing rain for your city,

OR

learn wind-listening to carry your prayers across continents?

❦ Reflection ❦

Scale and element shape impact—do you feel called to tend the local field or the global sky?

Would you rather...

Spend one moon cycle barefoot on earth each dawn,

OR

one moon cycle journaling beside running water each dusk?

~ Reflection ~

Grounding and flow train different muscles of presence—when do you meet yourself most honestly?

Would you rather...

Let mountains teach patience by hiking the same trail weekly,

OR

let rivers teach surrender by sitting at the same bend daily?

⁕ Reflection ⁕

Stability and movement are both teachers—what lesson is missing from your rhythm right now?

Would you rather...

Tend a community garden that feeds neighbors,

OR

restore a neglected patch of land that feeds wildlife?

Reflection

Service to people and service to ecosystem both nourish—where do you feel most responsible to show up?

Would you rather...

Carry a pocket of native seeds to scatter wherever you go,

OR

carry a small bag to remove litter wherever you go?

ʕ Reflection ʔ

Creation and clearing are twin devotions—which form of stewardship energizes you?

Would you rather...

Ask the soil for one lesson before every meal,

OR

thank the sky for one insight before every sleep?

∽ Reflection ∾

Gratitude can be rooted or spacious—where does your awe naturally begin?

Would you rather...

Sense the lay of ley lines beneath your feet,

OR

sense the mycelial conversations beneath a forest?

~ Reflection ~

Planetary grids and living networks reveal different maps—what kind of web helps you navigate?

Would you rather...

Keep a bowl of ocean water on your altar to remember vastness,

OR

a jar of local earth to remember belonging?

❦ Reflection ❧

Transcendence and rootedness balance the heart—what reminder steadies your choices?

Would you rather...

Partner with a humble field stone to anchor calm in your workspace,

OR

partner with a houseplant to teach daily tending?

~ Reflection ~

Stillness and care are practices—what disrupts your stress cycle more reliably?

Would you rather...

Map your year by solstices and equinoxes,

OR

by first blossom, first birdsong, and first frost?

～ Reflection ～

Cosmic timing and phenology both attune awareness—what calendar tunes you best?

Would you rather...

Sing to the morning birds for a week,

OR

hum to the evening crickets for a week?

~ Reflection ~

Dawn and dusk invite different nervous-system states—when do you receive harmony more easily?

Would you rather...

Drink only water you bless first,

OR

walk only routes where you can touch a tree each day?

❧ Reflection ☙

Micro-rituals rewire identity—what daily gesture would keep you consciously connected?

Chapter 7:
Cosmic Connection & Universal Wisdom

Would you rather...

Hold a conversation with the consciousness of the Milky Way for three minutes,

OR

decode the journey of a single photon from star to skin?

ᖇ Reflection ᖘ

Macro perspective or microscopic wonder—which lands wisdom more vividly for you now?

Would you rather...

Borrow the cosmic librarian's index to find any lesson in the Akashic field,

⊕R

the cosmic cartographer's map to navigate parallel timelines?

ᛋ Reflection ᛉ

Indexes and maps grant different agency—which tool would you use more responsibly?

Would you rather...

Receive one universal principle as a formula you can test,

OR

as a myth you can live into?

❧ Reflection ☙

Proof calms doubt; story animates courage—which form would actually guide your actions?

Would you rather...

Sit in a silence so deep you hear space hum,

OR

in a song so pure it folds the room into stillness?

◈ Reflection ◈

Sound and silence both carry truth—what setting unlocks your deepest listening?

Would you rather...

Share tea with a wise extraterrestrial anthropologist,

OR

share tea with your future descendant visiting from a healed Earth?

✦ Reflection ✦

Distant kin and future kin mirror us differently—whose eyes would change your practice faster?

Would you rather...

Carry a tuning fork that harmonizes groups into coherence,

OR

a prism that reveals hidden motives as colors?

～ Reflection ～

Coherence and discernment serve compassion differently—what kind of seeing serves your service?

Would you rather...

Attune to a sixty-second coherence window that sharpens decisions,

OR

schedule one annual leap window that reorders your path?

✣ Reflection ✣

Frequent course corrections or rare transformative leaps—which rhythm suits your nervous system?

Would you rather...

Understand sacred geometry in dreams,

OR

prime-number messages in waking visions?

❧ Reflection ☙

Symbols and numbers are two cosmic alphabets—which one is already whispering to you?

Would you rather...

Receive starseed memories with perfect clarity,

R

Earthseed instructions for community building with perfect clarity?

Reflection

Cosmic identity and grounded instructions offer different nourishment—what does your life hunger for?

Would you rather...

Catch a message written in aurora light,

OR

in the branching pattern of far-off lightning?

~ Reflection ~

Awe writes quickly on the heart—where does your attention feel most teachable?

Would you rather...

Feel the instant two strangers' choices tilt the collective timeline,

OR

never feel it but trust your small act contributed?

⚘ Reflection ⚘

Feeling impact can inspire; trusting impact can mature—what do you need to stay devoted?

Would you rather...

Learn to amplify fields where synchronicity clusters for everyone nearby,

OR

learn to dissolve fields where fear is contagious?

❥ Reflection ❥

Creating fields is stewardship—are you more called to amplify harmony or neutralize fear?

Chapter 8:
Self-Discovery & Conscious Creation

Would you rather...

Replace a limiting belief overnight with one catalytic ceremony,

OR

rewrite it gradually with a tiny daily practice for forty days?

✤ Reflection ✤

Fast transformation and steady rewiring both work—which path would you actually complete?

Would you rather...

Start each morning with a three-minute intention practice,

OR

start each week with a thirty-minute deep reset?

✌ Reflection ✌

Frequency and depth build momentum differently—which rhythm keeps you honest?

Would you rather...

Choose your next identity by a sentence you repeat aloud,

OR

by a boundary you refuse to break?

❦ Reflection ❧

Words declare; actions anchor—which builds more self-trust for you right now?

Would you rather...

See your most aligned future self vividly for sixty seconds,

OR

feel their steadiness in your body for six hours?

❧ Reflection ❧

Vision excites; embodiment integrates—which do you need to move from insight to action?

Would you rather...

Build a habit stack that hooks into something you already do,

OR

redesign your environment so the habit happens almost by itself?

~ Reflection ~

Willpower and architecture are both tools—which makes change feel effortless, not punishing?

Would you rather...

Ask one brave question every day,

OR

make one brave request every week?

⁓ Reflection ⁓

Curiosity opens doors; requests walk you through—which edge would mature you faster?

Would you rather...

Choose a single word to guide your year,

OR

choose a symbol and let it teach you in unexpected ways?

✤ Reflection ✤

Language focuses; symbol surprises—which fuel does your creativity crave?

Would you rather...

Reparent your inner critic into a useful coach,

OR

put it on a thirty-day sabbatical with love?

❧ Reflection ☙

Transmutation and timeout both protect your peace—which can your nervous system welcome now?

Would you rather...

Practice radical honesty with yourself for twenty-four hours,

OR

radical self-compassion for twenty-four hours?

～ Reflection ～

Truth without tenderness can sting; tenderness without truth can stall—which medicine is underdosed?

Would you rather...

Say "no" to one perfectly good option each day,

OR

say "yes" to one small stretch each day?

✤ Reflection ✤

Boundaries create space; courage fills it—which muscle needs training?

Would you rather...

Plan your next ninety days using measurable metrics,

OR

craft them using desired feelings as your compass?

ଛ Reflection ଛ

Numbers reassure; feelings align—which keeps you accountable without crushing joy?

Would you rather...

Celebrate every micro-win with a ten-second victory cue,

OR

celebrate only major milestones with a day-long retreat?

❧ Reflection ☙

Frequent reinforcement and rare intensives both motivate—which will sustain you longer?

Chapter 9:

Time, Legacy & Identity

Would you rather...

Be known by name to one soul across lifetimes,

OR

be unknown while your work quietly improves a million lives?

❧ Reflection ☙

Intimacy and scale seed different kinds of meaning—which legacy feels truer to you?

Would you rather...

Rewind the last five minutes to choose different words once a week,

OR

fast-forward healing so a mistake integrates overnight?

෨ Reflection ଔ

Do you want power over moments or over momentum—which would mature you more?

Would you rather...

Bury a time capsule with one object and one question,

OR

start a tradition others will keep long after you're gone?

✧ Reflection ✧

Artifacts and rituals both carry values—which will transmit yours more faithfully?

Would you rather...

Remember every kindness you received in vivid detail,

OR

every kindness you offered?

Reflection

Gratitude and accountability shape character differently—where does your attention belong?

Would you rather...

Stretch each day to feel twice as spacious when you're present,

OR

become effortlessly on time for everything forever?

❦ Reflection ❧

Spaciousness nurtures creativity; reliability builds trust—what do you need most now?

Would you rather...

Keep one consistent identity in every room,

OR

express distinct facets with different roles and communities?

✎ Reflection ✎

Coherence and adaptability both honor truth—how do you define authenticity?

Would you rather...

Choose your epitaph now in seven words,

OR

adopt a living motto you must revise every year?

✑ Reflection ✑

Fixing a meaning can focus; updating it can free—what serves your evolution?

Would you rather...

Hear your life story told by someone who misunderstood you,

OR

by someone who adored you?

❦ Reflection ❧

Projection and praise both distort—how will you anchor self-definition beyond either?

Would you rather...

Preserve your journals sealed for a future reader,

OR

burn them and keep only what you can embody?

❧ Reflection ☙

Archives and embodiment are two forms of memory—which feels more honest?

Would you rather...

Lose every photograph of you but keep every impact you made,

OR

keep every photograph but lose the record of your impacts?

❦ Reflection ❦

Image and consequence rarely weigh the same—which matters on your final ledger?

Would you rather...

Instantly know the one habit your descendants will thank you for starting,

OR

the one pattern they'll thank you for ending?

Reflection

Creation and cessation are both gifts—where is your leverage?

Would you rather...

Be remembered for courage when you were afraid,

OR

for kindness when you were hurt?

❦ Reflection ❧

Which virtue, practiced under pressure, best represents who you are becoming?

Chapter 10:
Spiritual Service & Mission

Would you rather...

Offer a monthly free clinic with short sessions,

OR

build a self-guided resource library that anyone can use anytime?

❧ Reflection ☙

Presence creates access now; infrastructure scales access later—what serves your community best this season?

Would you rather...

Create a quiet sanctuary space in your town,

travel as a pop-up practitioner bringing care to underserved places?

❦ Reflection ❧

Roots and reach shape impact differently—where does your service truly belong?

Would you rather...

Share your teachings under your own name to model visibility,

OR

publish under a collective to center community over personality?

∽ Reflection ∾

Personal brand and shared banner both carry responsibility—what message do you want your structure to send?

Would you rather...

Present channeled messages exactly as received,

OR

translate them into practical steps and everyday language?

❧ Reflection ☙

Purity preserves nuance; translation widens the doorway—what will help more people, more ethically?

Would you rather...

Keep strict session hours to protect your energy,

OR

answer occasional after-hours nudges when Spirit insists?

~ Reflection ~

Boundaries and flexibility both serve integrity—where is your healthy edge?

Would you rather...

Accept only clients who feel deeply aligned and ready,

OR

welcome curious skeptics willing to learn?

ꕥ Reflection ꕤ

Safety and bridge-building are both sacred—what can you hold without resentment or burnout?

Would you rather...

Set low fees to maximize access,

OR

charge premium rates and fund generous scholarships?

❧ Reflection ☙

Accessibility and sustainability are partners—
how will you balance them without self-sacrifice?

Would you rather...

Focus your work on crisis stabilization,

OR

dedicate it to long-term integration and growth?

Reflection

Urgency saves the moment; stewardship changes the arc—where are your gifts most effective?

Would you rather...

Document outcomes through rigorous data and case studies,

OR

gather narratives and art that reflect lived transformation?

~ Reflection ~

Evidence convinces the mind; story persuades the heart—what kind of proof would elevate your mission?

Would you rather...

Sign a public ethics pledge and publish your standards,

OR

keep a private vow you review and renew each month?

❧ Reflection ☙

Accountability outward and inward both matter—where do you most need reinforcement?

Would you rather...

Build a weekly circle that anchors consistent local support,

OR

host a global circle that meets across time zones asynchronously?

❦ Reflection ❦

Reliability and inclusivity ask different designs—what rhythm can you sustain with care?

Would you rather...

Choose one cause to devote the next ten years to,

OR

follow intuitive assignments that change each season?

ৎ Reflection ෫

Focus and adaptability are both forms of devotion—what path will keep you faithful and alive?

A Thank You from Lewis

From my heart to yours—thank you.
Thank you for saying yes to deeper reflection, for playing with possibility, and for trusting me to guide your inner dialogue with a blend of insight and humor. If these dilemmas helped you feel more peaceful, more curious, more you—then this book has done its job.

Your voice might be the exact spark someone else needs. If a question made you laugh, think, or heal, share a snippet—your choice, your why, or a photo of your journal—using #DeeperReflectionsWYR. Add a line about what shifted for you and tag the friends you'd love to explore with.

Please keep journaling. Keep asking bold questions. Share your insights with the friends who walk beside you. And if you'd like to go further—into clarity, healing, or intuitive development—I'd be honored to meet you in a private reading at www.lewismabee.com.

May your path be steady, your laughter frequent, and your intuition bright.
With gratitude beyond words,
Lewis

About the Author

Lewis Mabee is a psychic medium, healer, and spiritual educator whose work blends grounded guidance with a sense of wonder. Known for his warmth, accuracy, and uplifting humor, Lewis helps seekers reconnect with their intuition, understand energetic patterns, and make practical, heart-led choices in daily life.

Whether he's reading for a client, teaching a group, or crafting soul-stretching prompts, Lewis approaches spirituality as a living conversation—one where curiosity, compassion, and ethics lead the way. His Spiritual Dilemmas series grew from countless sessions and circles where a single brave question opened the door to deeper clarity, healing, and connection.

When he's not writing or working with clients around the world, you'll find him enjoying quiet moments of reflection, jotting synchronicities into a well-worn journal, or laughing with the people who keep him anchored and inspired. To book a reading or explore more of his work, visit www.lewismabee.com.

Resources & Next Steps

- Keep the momentum going
- Daily Practice: Choose 1 dilemma each morning; write a 3-line reflection and 1 action: "Because of this, I will…"
- Weekly Circle: Gather friends, pick 3 dilemmas, and use the Circle Agreements.
- Deepening Skills: Explore intuition journaling, breath work, and grounding after each session.

Work with Lewis: Book a private reading, join a workshop, or invite Lewis to your event.
Visit: www.lewismabee.com.

One Small Favor that Helps Immensely

If this book made you laugh, think, or feel more connected, would you leave a short review on Amazon?
Your words help other seekers find Spiritual Dilemmas: Deeper Reflections and keep this work going. Thank you!

Stay Connected

Follow along for new prompts, events, and behind-the-scenes:
- Instagram: @lewismabee
- Facebook: Lewis Mabee Spiritual

Love this book? Check out Lewis's other titles in the Spiritual Dilemmas series (and more) wherever you get your books.

www.ingramcontent.com/pod-product-compliance
Lightning Source LLC
Chambersburg PA
CBHW050329010526
44119CB00050B/725